Introduction

It is particularly appropriate that the National Trust for Scotland should have assumed, on behalf of Glasgow City Council, the management of Pollok House, where it is believed inaugural discussions about the founding of the conservation charity took place in 1931. Sir John Stirling Maxwell, owner of the house at that time, was a founder member of the Trust. In 1939 Sir John concluded with the Trust its first conservation agreement, securing the Nether Pollok estate for ever 'for the benefit of the citizens of Glasgow'.

The Trust's intention is to recreate the interiors of the house as they were at that time, when a small group of prominent Scots gathered in the smoking room (now the Cedar Room) to consider the establishment of a body to safeguard their country's built and natural heritage.

Above: the Maxwell coat-of-arms, from a watercolour of *c*1820 (Crown Copyright RCAHMS).

The Maxwells of Pollok

The Maxwell family is known to have been established at Pollok from the mid-thirteenth century. They also owned, in addition to this area, a changing permutation of other lands south of the River Clyde, gained or given as dowry. Originally, Nether Pollok was part of the Barony of the Mearns. 'Nether' means 'lower' and 'Pollok' is thought to mean 'a small pool in a sluggish river'. Upper Pollok, also within the Barony, is now the area around Newton Mearns.

The first Sir John Maxwell of Nether Pollok is recorded as living in the area in 1269. He is said to have been a great-grandson of Maccus, a Saxon who fled England after the Norman Conquest and

first settled near Kelso, where there is a spring known as Maccus' Well (the origin of 'Maxwell').

Successive lairds were knights until 1630 when Sir John Maxwell – bearing the traditional first name of the eldest son – was created 1st Baronet by Charles I. As he had no male children and was succeeded by his cousin, the baronetcy lapsed until 1682, when Charles II initiated the 1st Baronet of the second creation.

Sir John, the 1st Baronet second creation, became Lord Pollok as Lord Justice Clerk in 1699, but that title became extinct as he was succeeded by his cousin, the 2nd Baronet. This laird commissioned the building of the present Pollok House in 1747: it is thought that it was completed in 1752, only weeks before his death. His son, the 3rd Baronet, built the stone bridge over the River Cart near the house.

The baronetcy continued in the family and by 1844 the 8th Baronet was again a Sir John Maxwell, who had travelled widely in his youth and was active in the commercial expansion of Glasgow. Since he died childless in 1865, the baronetcy passed to his nephew, William Stirling of Keir, who took the name Sir William Stirling Maxwell.

Sir William had already won a considerable reputation for his writings on Spanish art and his major collection of Spanish and other paintings,

drawings and printed books. He died in 1878 leaving his two sons of 12 and 10 orphans, as his two wives had predeceased him.

The two boys were brought up by an aunt until the elder, Sir John Stirling Maxwell, came of age in 1887. His father had provided for his estates to be divided equally between the boys. Sir John inherited the baronetcy and chose the estates of Pollok, while his younger brother Archibald fell heir to the Stirling family lands at Keir, outside Dunblane.

An estate on the outskirts of an expanding city such as Glasgow was a major asset and Sir John had the income to expand the house to provide modern comforts. Well known in the community at large, Sir John's wide interests ranged over art, architecture, archaeology, forestry and gardening. He was a co-founder of the National Trust for Scotland in 1931.

After living in Pollok House for nearly seventy years, Sir John died in 1956, within one week of his ninetieth birthday. In 1966 his daughter Mrs Anne Maxwell Macdonald, the 11th Baronet, gifted Pollok House and the Stirling Maxwell Collection to the City of Glasgow, together with 146 hectares (361 acres) of the estate. In 1998 management of Pollok House was passed to the National Trust for Scotland by the City. The 700-year link with the family continues, as they retain accommodation in the house for their use when in Glasgow.

The Trust is creating a Family Room in the Alcove Bedchamber to give visitors a better understanding of the family history.

Opposite page, clockwise from top left: Sir John Maxwell, later Lord Pollok (1648-1732) by Sir John Baptist Medina (c1659-1710); engraving of Sir William Stirling Maxwell, 1891, from the frontispiece of his *Collected Works*; Sir John Maxwell, 8th Baronet (1791-1865) by an unknown artist of the British School; detail of engraving of Pollok House by J Denholm, c1796 (Glasgow Museums).
This page, top: Sir John Stirling Maxwell, 10th Baronet (1866-1956) in shooting costume at Pollok, 1929, by William Ranken (1881-1941); bottom: Sir John in his sitting room at Pollok House, 1955 (*Scottish Field* magazine).

The History and Architecture of Pollok House

By tradition the Maxwell family built three successive castles in this area before the present house. With little archaeological evidence it is difficult to be accurate, but the motte at the top of the rhododendron walk, now surmounted by an ancient beech tree, and a part of the stable courtyard indicate probable locations.

By the 1740s the family needed to replace the last castle, built in the late fourteenth century, with a modern, fashionable home. The 2nd Baronet, Sir John Maxwell (1686-1752), was sufficiently prosperous to contemplate this major change. He selected a site on higher ground to the west of the old building, probably to escape the worst of the river flooding.

Although William Adam, the pre-eminent architect in Scotland at the time, is said to have supplied a plan in 1737, evidence for this has since disappeared. Sir John Stirling Maxwell believed that the house was designed by Adam: but the plan as executed reflects mid-eighteenth-century ideas in its paired dining room and drawing room across a central lobby, and this feature, in common with the spinal corridors, makes it most unlikely that an earlier William Adam design was followed. By this time there were several competent local architects in Glasgow.

Work did not begin on the new house until 1747, a delay which may have been due to an immediate shortage of money, but which allowed the involvement of Sir John's eldest son John, the 3rd Baronet, recently returned from his Grand Tour of Europe. The house as built was on a compact scale, with four floors plus attics, and 80ft-long main façades. Its exterior is sober, almost austere, enlivened by two pairs of sculptured swags on the south façade and the classical pedimented entrance door.

The interior is much more exuberant – an effect achieved by the ornate plasterwork throughout the principal rooms. By the time he wrote his history of Scottish architecture, *Shrines and Homes of Scotland*, Sir John had deduced from stylistic comparison with Blair Castle that the plasterwork at Pollok House was by the Clayton family. The Claytons were responsible for similarly energetic plasterwork at the nearby Hamilton Palace. But unfortunately no papers survive to confirm this, or to document any of the building, decoration and furnishing at Pollok.

Opposite page, clockwise from top left: a garden pavilion, one of the 1903 additions; the Dining Room (now the Drawing Room) in 1913 (*Country Life* Picture Library); the front entrance to the house in *c*1870, with the porte-cochère that was later replaced by the entrance hall (Annan Gallery, Glasgow); the Maxwell shield in the pediment above the main door.

In 1865 the 8th Baronet was succeeded by his nephew, Sir William Stirling Maxwell. With other houses and a busy life principally in London, he took little interest in Pollok. These quiet years for the house continued until 1888. Sir William's elder son, John, had become 10th Baronet in 1878 but as a minor he had lived with his aunt. In 1887 he came of age and was allowed to choose which of his father's estates he should inherit. He selected Pollok, as its proximity to the booming industrial centre of Glasgow made it very valuable.

Although there had been some minor nineteenth-century

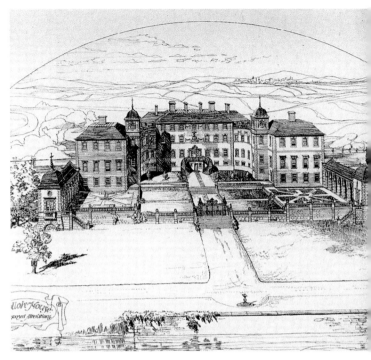

changes to Pollok, Sir John inherited the original house more or less intact because his father's attentions had been lavished on Keir in Stirlingshire, the other family seat. Pollok's diminutive eighteenth-century scale was not, however, conducive to late Victorian and Edwardian ideas of comfort and country-house entertaining.

Sir John commissioned the eminent Edinburgh architect Robert Rowand Anderson (1834-1921) to make extensive additions to Pollok while preserving, with his characteristic flair and sympathy, the eighteenth-century idiom. Spacious new interiors were needed to house Sir John's share of his father's collection of Spanish paintings and the Keir library. A new entrance hall and basement office wing, in keeping with these ambitions, were begun in 1890. But the successive plans drawn up in the early 1900s, among Anderson's office drawings now in Edinburgh University library, betray a degree of indecision.

It seems likely, as the bird's-eye perspective vividly demonstrates,

that Sir John came to realise that these inflated additions could not but destroy the charm of the original house. The executed design, therefore, took the form of tactful single-storey pavilions which, in retrospect, are an early indication of the modern conservationist principles that Sir John was to promote in later life. Aesthetics triumphed over modern comforts in Sir John's decision to retain the eighteenth-century drawing and dining rooms as his principal reception rooms. Anderson faithfully copied the style of the old in his new work. Although a handsome new Library was created in the eastern pavilion, the large Spanish pictures were perhaps never wholly at ease in these small-scale spaces.

Sir John and Anderson's work at Pollok is important because, with unusual thoroughness, they furnished these Georgian interiors with Chippendale furniture, building on a small nucleus of Pollok's original eighteenth-century contents. Pollok was thus unusual in Scotland in pioneering a taste for the neo-Georgian style.

Opposite page, top right: Robert Rowand Anderson's early drawing for the extension of Pollok House, showing the initial plan for two huge wings that was later discarded (reproduced by permission of Edinburgh University Library; Crown Copyright RCAHMS); bottom left: Building work in progress, *c*1905 (Glasgow Museums).
This page: carving the gatepost lions in Hew Lorimer's studio at Kellie, 1950 (Glasgow Museums).

Tour of the House

The Entrance Hall

Today's visitors enter the house, just as they would have done over a hundred years ago, by the grand entrance hall, which Sir John added in 1890, replacing the utilitarian Victorian porte-cochère with a corrugated iron roof. The hall's main purpose is to provide access to the house with the minimum of exposure to the worst of the Scottish weather.

The materials used in the new hall were sumptuous, combining the finest mahogany and marble with glitteringly bevelled glass. The unusual format of stairs connects the various floor levels while providing cloakroom facilities for guests in the lower entrance hall.

Originally the wall was panelled in polished mahogany up to the height of the windows, a style in keeping with the planned major expansion of the house. When these plans were reduced in scale after 1900, the rest of the house was decorated in plaster rather than carved wood, and the hall must have seemed heavy, almost baroque, in comparison to the rococo feel of the decoration elsewhere. Accordingly the polished wood was painted out soon after the pavilions were completed in 1908.

The hall retains the mahogany furniture in the Chippendale style, attributed to Whytock & Reid. The octagonal table in the middle of the floor displays a map showing a radius of 50 miles around Pollok House. When central heating was installed the table became a cover for a centrally placed radiator. The carved side tables are curved to fit the apsidal shape of the entrance hall.

The staircase, with its ranks of family portraits, is a vantage point from which to see the display of armorial shields showing the arms of family, friends and neighbours around the cornice of the hall. The great lantern hanging from the ceiling is copied from a design in Chippendale's *Gentleman and Cabinet Maker's Director*, published in 1754. Planned with electricity in mind, every second glass panel slides upwards to allow bulbs to be changed.

Busts of Sir William Stirling Maxwell and his first wife stand guard either side of the doorway – originally the front door – that leads through into the rest of the house. With characteristic sensitivity, Rowand Anderson moved the original stone door casing to ground level, to form the new front door to the hall extension. Through the magnificent mahogany doors with bevelled glass and ormolu fittings the visitor enters the main corridor.

San Ildefonso receiving the chasuble, 1770, by Juan de Paez

The Corridor

The original entrance hall and the garden lobby beyond were probably linked together to form the central corridor by Anderson, who carefully reproduced the original details of the Ionic order. He also designed the fireplace further up the corridor on the left, facing the main staircase, and retained the other mid-nineteenth-century fireplace.

In the stairwell stands a remarkable piece of Scottish clockmaking – an astronomical clock by Craig of Glasgow, dated to 1764 and with the Maxwell family crest engraved on the dial. It is original to the house and has always stood in this corridor. As with any clock of this complexity it is unique, incorporating only what its first owner required. Sir John probably inherited the antiquarian furniture in the corridor from the family seat at Keir.

Boys playing at see-saw by Francisco de Goya (1746-1828); right: *Philip II of Spain*, c1570, by Alonso Sanchez Coello (1531/2-88).

Over the second fireplace hangs a painting of the Emperor Charles V, a contemporary copy of a picture lost in a fire in 1604.

To the left is a games table of 'mulberry wood' – not a species, but a process to colour and decorate a pale wood such as elm or maple. Opposite is a rare surviving portrait of Philip II by his favourite artist Sanchez Coello. Dating to c1570, the painting shows the king wearing a famous suit of armour, one of his most valuable possessions. The pendant portrays his fourth wife, Anne of Austria. Below these are two paintings of children's games by Goya (1746-1828), acquired in 1843.

The Music Room

At the end of the corridor, on the left, is the Music Room – the original drawing room in the eighteenth century and the most formal room in the house. The room takes its present name from the organ, formerly on the east wall, which was designed by Rowand Anderson.

The history of this room is complex. Sir James Caw's printed catalogue of the paintings at Pollok House, published in 1936, states that there was a fire in this room in 1908. The most important loss was a full-length portrait by Raeburn of Harriet, sister of the 8th Baronet, the most valuable item in the house when Sir John took possession in 1888.

Sir John copied the bold red colour on the walls following its success at the Wallace Collection, London, where he was chairman of trustees. The centre light, missing its globes, is a rare survivor of Rowand Anderson's upgrading of the fittings when electric light was installed. The pier tables on the window wall are recorded in the 1844 inventory, along with the two pairs of pier glasses, suggesting that they are probably original to the house

The Trust has restored the arrangement of pictures to approximate that adopted by Sir John Stirling Maxwell. Over the fireplace hangs a sixteenth-century version of Titian's *Christ carrying the Cross*, now in the Prado, Madrid, and formerly in the private oratory in the Escorial. Sir William's acquisition of this version of the painting emphasises his fascination with the artists who decorated this most refined and intellectual of Spanish palaces. On the corridor wall is *The Labours of Adam and Eve* by Alonso Cano (1601-67). The subject derives from a Netherlandish engraving. Cano's working life was dramatically interrupted when he was arrested and tortured – but never charged – after his wife's murder.

On the opposite wall hangs *An Allegory of Repentance* attributed to Antonio de Pereda y Salgado (1608-78). Heavy with symbolism, this is the most baroque painting in the collection, combining boldness of gesture, opulence of subject and exquisite painting.

Portrait of Anne Stirling Maxwell, later Dame Anne Maxwell Macdonald, 1910-11, by Sir William Nicholson (1872-1949).

The Print Room

This room connects the original house to the new pavilion, and initially contained the organ pipes. Its present name derives from the cabinet for solander (book-shaped) boxes of prints and drawings, built in the space that formerly housed the organ console.

The hanging shelves held part of the collection of emblem books acquired by Sir William and which Sir John bequeathed on his death to Glasgow University library. These books, published in the sixteenth and seventeenth centuries, depicted philosophical ideas in a figurative way – justice, for instance, as a blindfolded woman holding scales. Sir William was in the forefront of the early Victorian interest in symbolism.

Facing each other are portraits of Sir John Stirling Maxwell by William Ranken and of his daughter Anne, later Dame Anne Maxwell Macdonald (1905-2011), by Sir William Nicholson. The Ranken was painted between 9 and 14 August 1929, and is as much a portrait of Pollok House and the gardens as it is a likeness of Sir John.

The Library

The Library occupies the whole of the eastern pavilion. It was the most important interior to be added by Sir John and is probably the finest twentieth-century library in Scotland. When he arrived at Pollok Sir John found nearly 3,000 books – the number rose to 7,000 when his share of his father's library from Keir was added – and provision for accommodating these was an important part of his specification to Rowand Anderson.

The room echoes the Corridor, being divided into compartments – in this case three – by pairs of Ionic columns. The two chimneypieces were

designed to show the El Greco paintings – *Portrait of a Man* (*c*1590) and *The Lady in a Fur Wrap* (*c*1577-9), easily the best known and best loved painting in the collection.

The middle compartment centres on the garden, reached through french windows, which open on to the Library parterre. This compartment is also in line with the start of the rhododendron walk leading up the ridge towards the original motte of one of the family's earlier castles.

Photographs of the Library in *Country Life* of 1913 show basket arches separating the compartments. These were changed to the current segmental arches at some stage, presumably to strengthen them. The overall effect is orderly but sumptuous, with the contrast of the polished mahogany bookcases and the rest of the room painted old white.

At present furniture is sparse but the original intention was that the room be fully furnished. When Sir John had a stroke in 1940 and was confined to a wheelchair he used the Library as his main day room, allowing access to his beloved garden, and the Music Room as a bedroom. Since 1960 the Library has been a popular venue for chamber concerts, hence the grand piano. The concerts continue to thrive.

This page: paintings by El Greco in the Library. Left: *Lady in a Fur Wrap*, *c*1577-9; above: *Portrait of a Man*, *c*1590.
Opposite page, left to right: Silver gilt nautilus shell cup by Tobias Wolff of Nuremberg, 1622; George II coffee urn by James Ker, 1733; *Perseus Arming*, bronze statuette (cast *c*1905) by Sir Alfred Gilbert (1854-1734), creator of the *Eros* statue in London's Piccadilly Circus.

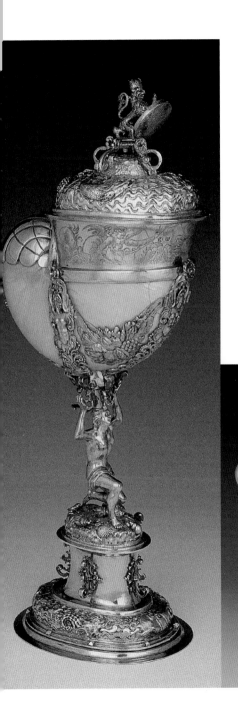

The Silver Corridor

Leaving the Library by the door opposite the french windows, the visitor enters the Silver Corridor. Originally known as the Library Lobby, its bookcases held the oversize books. In the 1970s these were modified to display cases for silver and other small objects. Today they hold a variety of objects, from ceramics to silver and miniatures.

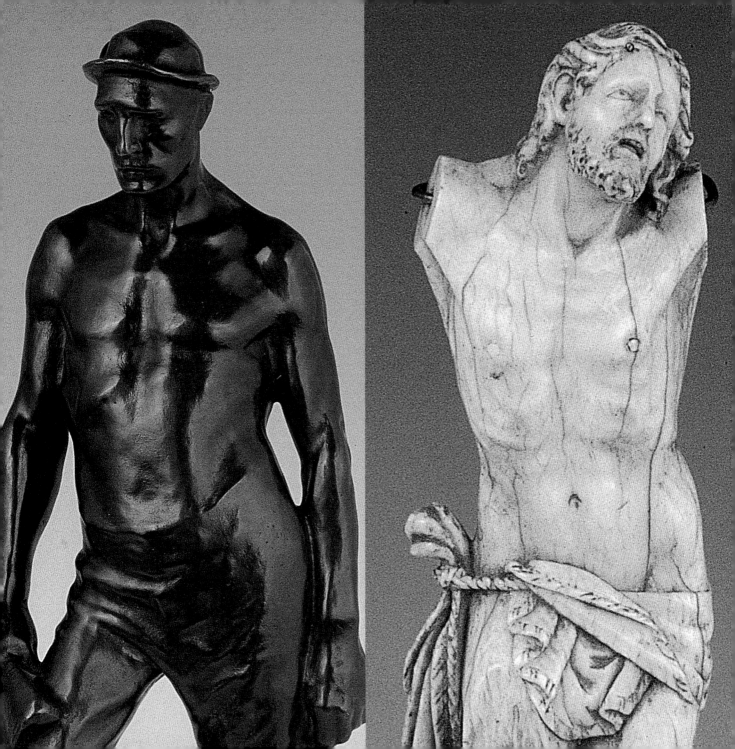

The Morning Room

Lady Stirling Maxwell used this as her private sitting room during the 1920s and 1930s. The room now has no decorative stucco, and the Siena marble chimneypiece dates from the mid-nineteenth century, when the room was a library.

The contrast is striking between the domestic scale of this room and the grandeur of the pictures on every wall – an array of royal and papal portraits, which served to project powerful political and dynastic images to foreign courts. Pope Clement VII, who refused Henry VIII his divorce, faces Henry's daughter Queen Elizabeth I. Over the fireplace is a full-length portrait of Charles II of Spain. The product of inbreeding to keep the dynasty pure, his tragic life was documented in a series of yearly portraits, of which this is one.

By crossing the main corridor the visitor comes to the Business Room.

Opposite page, left to right: *Miner*, a bronze statuette by Constantin Meunier (1831-1905); Flemish ivory crucifix of the eighteenth century. This page, top left: Derby porcelain flowerpot and stand, *c*1800, one of a pair; bottom left: *Pope Clement VII* (in office 1523-34) by the Studio of Sebastiano del Piombo (*c*1485-1547).

The Business Room

This room retains its original stucco work and is one of the most attractive in the house. Of particular note are the *trompe-l'oeil* bust over the elaborate fireplace and the rare pier glass in stucco topped by a basket of flowers. The fitted green carpet is a copy of the one laid here during Sir John's lifetime.

It was from here – originally known as the Work Room – that Sir John managed the gardens and the estate and painted his

Lady Stirling Maxwell by Sir James Guthrie (1908).

watercolours. His keen interest in horticulture is evident from the volumes in the built-in bookcase. Sir John's desk always occupied this position, as did the two Raeburn armchairs beside the fire. The glass paste medallions by James Tassie on either side of the fireplace were introduced by Sir John to remind visitors that Tassie was born nearby in Pollokshaws.

The flower painting by William Ranken, over the fireplace, is based on an arrangement by Lady Stirling Maxwell using the two Batavian ware Chinese pots on display elsewhere in the room.

The large portrait from 1908 is of Lady Stirling Maxwell by a family friend, Sir James Guthrie, President of the Royal Scottish Academy. The unfinished portrait

Christ and the Pope, by an unknown German artist of the sixteenth century

The Dining Room Corridor

This corridor forms part of the original layout of the house, providing a servants' area at right angles to the main corridor. It widens out as part of the link to the pavilion.

Here are an early Murillo, *Madonna and Child with St John*, called 'The Peasant Madonna' because of her peasant fringed shawl, and *Adoration of the Magi* by Luis Tristán, who worked with El Greco.

Madonna and Child with St John, c1645-50, by Bartolomé Estebán Murillo (1617-82)

of the 8th Baronet is by Raeburn. Probably the last painting he worked on, it is dated to 1822 although it did not enter the collection until 1877 when Sir William acquired it from Raeburn's descendants. The paper label, closely hand-written, is typical of Sir William's method of recording.

Beneath the portrait is an unusual German painting

dating to the sixteenth century, contrasting the humility and poverty of Christ with the self-aggrandisement of the Pope.

Balancing this is one of the most loved paintings in the house, *Girl with a Dove* (left) by Anton Raffael Mengs (1728-79). It is in a style of frame much used by Sir William.

The Dining Room

Rowand Anderson designed this as a billiard room, forming a balance to the Library in the

western pavilion. But at the outbreak of the First World War it became a ward of the auxiliary hospital for officers based in the house, and the billiard table was moved out into the Library. After the war, this room became first a sitting room and then the Dining Room.

It was given its special character in 1942 when Sir John introduced the large-scale Dutch hunting scenes by Gerrit Malleyn (1753-1816), which were framed by Scott Morton & Co to read as part of the architecture of the room.

The Trust commissioned copies of the original walnut Chippendale Gothick dining chairs from Charles Taylor of Dalkeith, and brought back into this room the eighteenth-century pier tables and the Adam-style sideboard in the positions selected by Sir John.

24

Above: *Sir Jeffrey Chaucer and the nine and twenty pilgrims on their journey to Canterbury* (1808) by William Blake (1757-1827).
Opposite page, left: Blake's *Adam naming the beasts* (1810).

The Cedar Room

This smoking room was created in 1929, as the inlaid wall panel records, from the service room for the Dining Room next door. Originally there were sinks at the window and a dumb waiter to transport food from the kitchens in the basement. It was panelled by the estate carpenter, using wood from North Borneo.

The fireplace retains the V-shaped form of bricks used by Sir John to improve the heat output from logs.

The room contains some of the major paintings in the collection. The series of William Blake paintings was acquired in 1853 from the estate of one of his few patrons, at a time when the artist's reputation was at a nadir.

Early discussions about the formation of the National Trust for Scotland took place in this room.

The Drawing Room

This was designed as the dining room, as shown by the riotous stucco depictions of the chase and motifs such as seashells, as well as the original buffet recess. Sir John tried to use the room for its original purpose but found it inadequate by twentieth-century standards. Once the Dining Room was moved to the west pavilion this room was used as the principal living room of the house.

The eighteenth-century buffet displays part of the maiolica collection of Sir William and Sir John. The portraits of major historical figures, poets and Jacobites were collected by Sir William. Only a very small part of his collection is represented here.

The large red Turkey rug formerly in this room has been rewoven.

The Staircase and Upper Landing

The principal staircase in the house extends only from the ground to the first floor. Access to all the other floors – including the secondary bedrooms and the schoolroom/nursery – is from a service stair that runs from basement to attic (not open to the public).

The grand sweep of the main staircase, punctuated by two alcoves, is hung with portraits, chiefly of the Hapsburgs. The image of Philip IV supported by putti, by Martinez de Gradilla (died 1673) hangs above the portrait of the king's brother, the Cardinal Infante Ferdinand, by Gaspard de Crayer (1584-1669?).

Over the fireplace on the upper landing is the portrait of a royal baby. Its pathetic regality either appeals to or horrifies most onlookers.

The adjoining corridor is hung with watercolours by Sir John Stirling Maxwell, who won prizes for his painting at Eton and became a prolific artist. He donated these works to the Trust, and they have now found their way home.

The Keir Bedroom and Dressing Room

Previously known by the family as the Red Bedroom, this was the principal guest room at Pollok. Sir John and Lady Stirling Maxwell's private suite was at the opposite end of this floor. The room boasts magnificent Chinese wallpaper dating to *c*1800, rescued from Keir, conserved and installed here by Glasgow Museums in 1991. The Scottish chrysanthemum flat-woven carpet is on loan from the family.

The Trust has introduced furniture in the eighteenth-century style to give visitors the impression of a Pollok bedroom.

The adjoining Dressing Room, painted to match, displays an expanding hang of photographs, maps and images of Keir and Pollok.

Opposite page: the Keir bedroom retains many rare decorative features. Left: rare manganese fireplace tiles, *c*1755, from the Delftfield Pottery in Glasgow; right: Chinese wallpaper, *c*1800.

Boys playing at soldiers by Francisco de Goya (1746-1828).

The Family Room

The Alcove Bedroom has been turned into a Family Room showing portraits of recent members of the family as well as earlier paintings and general memorabilia. The model of Crookston Castle, as the plaque records, was made by G Finlay in 1827, by tradition of 'Queen Mary's yew', the tree under which Mary, Queen of Scots, is supposed to have sheltered during the battle of Langside in 1568. Crookston Castle was gifted to the Trust by Sir John Stirling Maxwell in 1931, and became its first property.

The family have lent back the scrapbooks dating to the 1820s and 1830s and created by Lady Maxwell, the wife of the 7th Baronet, who described them in a poem as 'turning a sad hour into a happy one'. The enormous albums – there are five in total – include a long series of watercolours of the house, gardens

and the wider estate, and reveal an amazingly vivid microcosm of early nineteenth-century Scotland through fashion plates, newspapers and royal memorabilia, each carefully cut out and pasted in to provide many quirky juxtapositions.

Sir William Stirling Maxwell and Spanish Art

Sir William Stirling Maxwell's collection, half of which remains at Pollok, can claim to be the most important collection of Spanish art ever formed in this country. More remarkable is the fact that it was collected by one man in just twenty years.

After unsuccessfully attempting to enter parliament, William Stirling Maxwell travelled extensively, reaching Spain in 1842. The country, its people and its history caught his imagination. He wrote his pioneering history of Spanish art, the three-volume *Annals of the Artists of Spain*, in 1848, a year after inheriting Keir and sufficient income to start collecting seriously.

The collection reflects a groundbreaking interest in the social history of art, highlighting the relationships between artist and patron and the struggle of Spanish artists to achieve a higher status. The remarkable group of portraits, including the Hapsburg rulers of Spain and the Spanish Netherlands, reflects Sir William's interest in portraits as historical records. In addition, he recognised the propaganda function of portraits in creating a particular image of the sitter.

Most significant of all, the collection contains examples by artists whose names were new in Britain at that date, Sir William being the first to collect and promote El Greco and Goya.

The Centre Room and Exhibition Space

The Centre Room was Lady Stirling Maxwell's sitting room, connected to her bedroom until she began increasingly to use the Morning Room. The room was planned as the library in the eighteenth century, and some of the shelving is original.

The room contains a display of Chinese and Japanese objects, examples of the everyday and luxury items that became available to households such as Pollok in the eighteenth century, as trade with the East expanded.

From time to time there will be temporary exhibitions in the adjoining room.

Visitors should now retrace their steps and descend from the Entrance Hall into the servants' quarters.

Ivory basket, *c*1800 and, inset bottom, late eighteenth-century miniature landscape, from the Sassoon Chinese ivory collection; inset top: Japanese Imari ceramic charger, *c*1700.

The Servants' Quarters

The central spine of the sophisticated domestic arrangements at Pollok is the Basement Corridor, running the full length of the service quarters. Laid out in 1900 from designs by Rowand Anderson, the basement provided space for an army of servants to carry out tasks, each in its designated location.

Left: The main kitchen, now the Edwardian Kitchen Restaurant. Opposite: the Still Room.

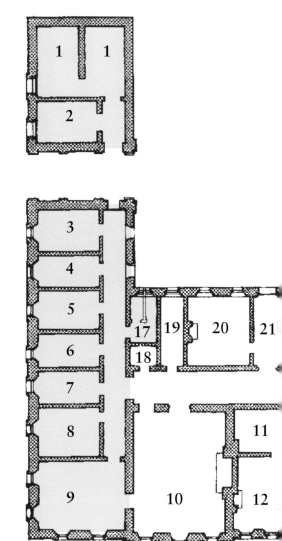

The domestic routine was organised around the butler, with his pantry, wine cellar and silver room; the housekeeper, with her still room (now the Food Shop) and linen room; and the cook with her main kitchen.

Today the kitchen area houses the restaurant and remains a centre of activity. The housekeeper's sitting room — originally a dining room for the more 'important' servants — is now the Trust gift shop.

At the opposite end of the corridor from the kitchen were the male servants' bedrooms. The female live-in servants had rooms in the attic floor — a full house apart.

Laundry facilities were elsewhere on the estate.

Above: the Dry Goods Store. Right: diagrammatic plan of the basement based on Rowand Anderson's original design.

34

1   Coal
2   Wood
3   Dairy
4   Vegetable Scullery
5   Fish and Cold Storage
6   Wet Meat and Game
7   Cook's Pantry
8   Cook's Room
9   Scullery
10 Kitchen
11 Drying Room
12 Brushing Room
13 Servants' Hall
14 Boots

15 Scullery
16 Cycles
17 WC
18 Press
19 Knives
20 Gunroom
21 Luggage Entrance
22 China Store
23 Dry Goods Store
24 Still Room
25 Store Room
26 Housekeeper's Room
27 Housekeeper's Bedroom
28 Linen Room

29 Butler's Room
30 Store
31 Housemaid's Pantry
32 Visitors' Valet
33 Butler's Bedroom
34 Boys' Room
35 Sir John's Valet
36 Footmen's Bedroom
37 Men-servants' Bathroom
38 Housemaids' Living Room
39 Lower Hall
40 Dark Room
41 Wine Cellar
42 Butler's Pantry

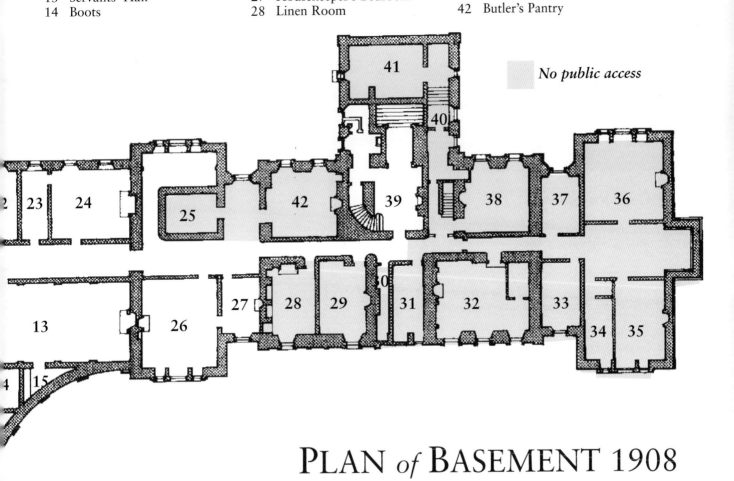

No public access

PLAN *of* BASEMENT 1908

Above right: the head gardener (with beard) and some of his staff, at Pollok in 1905.

The Gun Room

Next to the servants' quarters is the Gun Room, built around 1900. Pollok was a typical country estate with a wide range of game, particularly duck on the many surrounding ponds. The built-in cases can accommodate twenty firearms with provision for cartridges, equipment and cleaning kits underneath. Sir John got to know his future father-in-law, Sir Herbert Maxwell, on their many shooting and fishing expeditions – very much a male preserve.

The Gardens and the Wider Estate

The gardens seen today were created to complement Sir John Stirling Maxwell's expansion of Pollok House after 1890. As well as formal gardens, he introduced a woodland garden growing primarily rhododendrons. The 458 hectares (1,130 acres) of countryside and open space in the estate were the subjects of the conservation agreement Sir John entered into with the National Trust for Scotland in 1939. The 146 hectares (361 acres) that make up the Pollok Country Park contain the gardens, stable block and The Burrell Collection as well as Pollok House.